VIKING
BLOG PROFITS

Chapter 1:
Introduction

A blog is the best way to create custom content for your current and future customers. Chapter one of this book looks at how a blog can help your business, how to find good examples of business blogs, and how to decide what kind of content your blog should feature. Chapter two examines the platform options for blogging, how often you should post content, and the best ways to get your content to an audience. Chapter three tells you how to come up with content ideas, stick to a posting schedule, and earn some money through your blog. Whether you're thinking of starting a blog or want to grow an existing one, this guide will teach you all you need to know.

What is your most important source of customer interaction? For many businesses, it's their blog. If your business doesn't have a blog yet, you're missing out on a crucial stream of new customers, as well as increased revenue from existing customers. Let's look at a few statistics:

- Nearly 20 million people have blogs, taking up 23% of all internet usage.
- 81% of U.S. online consumers trust information and advice from blogs.
- 61% have made a purchase based on a blog recommendation.
- Small businesses that blog get 126% more lead growth, and B2B marketers who blog get 67% more lead growth than those who don't.

Whether your company is brand new or becoming established in the industry, a blog is an excellent resource. The sooner you set it up, the more time it will have to build credibility and an audience. A blog allows you to craft your brand's voice, improve SEO and reach more people by giving you content to share on social media.

By using your blog regularly, you can create timely and relevant posts and build a reputation as an industry thought leader. Blogs are easy to use and completely customisable, so you can create one that perfectly suits your business' needs.

Blogging is not something you need to figure out on your own. Because of the popularity of the platform, there are millions of blogs that you can read and draw inspiration from when creating your content. It might feel like a fine line between being inspired and stealing, but the key is to learn from the writing style and come up with your own stuff, not copy the content topics word for word. Just reading other business' blogs will improve your understanding of blogging, and you'll learn what does and doesn't work over time.

The best way to find helpful blogs is to think about why you're looking for them. If you need to learn more about developing a tone of voice, search for leading business blogs. If you want to see what blogging is like in your industry, search for industry leaders. If you want to figure out what kind of blogging you should be producing at this point in your company, search for your competitors' blogs. You'll find that one blog will lead to another and pretty soon, you'll have a whole list of blogs you can read and use to inspire your content.

Deciding what kind of blog you want to create can be difficult for a lot of people starting out. They wonder what topics they should and shouldn't write about, how broad or narrow they should be in terms of their niche, and how they should form the voice of their brand. The best way to figure out all of these things is to look at your target audience. You may think that what you blog about should be decided by your product, but it should actually be decided by your customers.

Look at your target audience and the kind of blog posts they're reading within your industry. Are they looking for product recommendations? Are they reading about current trends in your industry? When you learn what is being read, you'll learn what kind of content will drive traffic to your site. You can use tools like BuzzSumo and Alltop to discover the kind of topics that are doing well in your industry.

Chapter 2:

Where to Blog

It can be difficult to decide where to post your blog when there are so many options, so in this chapter, we're going to go through some of the best and most popular blogging platforms available.

Your website

If your company already has a website, the best place to have your blog will be alongside the rest of your content. Your website may be built on one of the other platforms in this list, so you'll see the benefits of those platforms in more detail.

Wordpress.org

Wordpress.org is the world's most popular blogging software. It's incredibly customisable, allowing you to add extra features like forums, online stores, and membership options. Many people use Wordpress to build sites other than blogs, so this is a great option if you plan to grow your blog into a full website later. It's free to use but you'll need to buy a domain name and web hosting. This software has a bit of a learning curve but overall is very easy to use, with thousands of plug-ins and themes available so you don't need to do any coding. When signing up, make sure you're on Wordpress.org and not

Wordpress.com, which is a site for smaller blogs with more limited options.

Wix

Wix is very easy to use with no coding experience, allowing you to design your blog with drag-and-drop tools. However, its free account is quite limited and it isn't completely customisable with issues such as limited third-party apps and not being able to change a design template once you've chosen it.

Blogger

Blogger is a free service that is owned by Google, meaning you get the advantage of Google's robust security and reliability. It's easy to use without technical knowledge, but it's quite limited in terms of design and you can't expand it into a multi-featured website if your business grows.

Squarespace

Squarespace is a paid platform that is very easy to use and has a great range of professionally-designed templates, but not many feature and integration options. Their Personal plan starts at $16/month and their Business plan starts at $26/month. Many bloggers end up switching from Squarespace to Wordpress to minimise their expenses and add more features to their website.

When you've chosen a platform and set up your blog, make sure to post regularly! Studies have shown that blogs that post every two or three days see the biggest increase in traffic. Companies that publish 16 or more blog posts per month get almost three and a half times more traffic than those who post four or less times a month. In companies of every size, posting 11 or more blog posts a month created at least double the traffic of those who rarely posted. If this seems daunting, don't worry; we'll discuss how to create this much content in the next chapter.

In order to get all these great blog posts to your audience, you need to use social media, email lists, and search engines to your advantage. Blog content is perfect for sharing on your existing social media accounts, as well as sending to your email lists. Use these opportunities to share your blog with your existing audience through media that allows them to share it with their friends.

When creating content, use search engine optimisation to your advantage by including keywords and backlinks in every post. That way, you'll come up top when a potential customer searches for the solution to a problem or question they have.

The best content for search engines and social media is to provide answers to questions customers are searching. You'll pick up customers on search engines with your SEO content and entice social media users with answers to questions they've been wondering for a while.

Chapter 3:

Blog Topics

Coming up with ideas for blog posts can seem difficult if you aren't used to creating content on a regular basis. However, once you get started, you can expand on your existing writing with more detail and update posts with new information. Here are some post ideas to get you started:

- Current trends or news in your industry

- Interview an expert (could be someone on your team)

- Point out common mistakes that users make

- How-to posts

- Guest posts from industry leaders

- Guides to buying the right product

- Answer frequently asked questions

- Beginner's guides for products

- Comparison of similar products

- Feature a customer success story

Each of these topics can be built upon and turned into a suite of posts that all reference one another. For example, a good post about frequently asked questions that is shared on social media will invite more questions in the comments- when you have enough questions, create a second post! Customers love to interact with content that relates to them, so make sure to encourage that by asking for their thoughts at the end of each blog.

Blogging can be pretty intensive, particularly if you want to post multiple times a week. There are many organisational tools such as Trello and Asana that can be used to keep you on a regular schedule. Some people like to write their posts one at a time according to their posting schedule, whereas others prefer to spend one or two days a month writing all their posts and then publishing from their cache. Some people just find that they don't have the time to blog on top of everything else they're doing within the business.

This can lead to some businesses not creating a blog at all, but blogs are such powerful resources that this should be avoided if at all possible. If you don't have the time to blog yourself, consider outsourcing to a freelance writer. Many companies do this with great results, and if you find the right freelancer, you can get all your content done without needing to hire a new person every time. Freelance writers will have the writing skills you may not have, as well as the time to do the work to a high standard.

If you're interested in earning money through your blog, there are a number of advertising styles you can implement on your site. Most options display ads on your site and the amount you earn is decided on the amount of views or clicks it receives. These options work best for high-traffic sites, and it's important that you consider how they will affect your readers' enjoyment.

A more subtle way to advertise is the use of affiliate links, which also allows you to only endorse brands that are relevant to your industry and that you believe in. In order to create an affiliate link, you need to reach out to a company and join their partner program, if they have one. Joining this program gives you a unique link ID that you include in your ads or blog posts. When a user clicks this link and buys the product, you receive a commission. Affiliate links and other advertising methods work best for large blogs, so this might be something you do in the future rather than right now, but don't be afraid to consider it if you're writing posts about specific products.

Blogging can be time-consuming and requires you to think creatively about the link between you and your customers. These might feel like large obstacles to some people, but the rewards of blogging for your business are so great that they will definitely outweigh the negatives you face in that initial learning curve. Regular blogging can double or even triple your website traffic, and informational pieces about your industry will create a strong brand voice that customers trust.

The key is to blog early and blog often, so use these tips and get started today!

www.ingramcontent.com/pod-product-compliance
Lightning Source LLC
Chambersburg PA
CBRC090852210326
41597CB00011B/174